Things I Have Kept

Denise Bennett

Published by Cinnamon Press
www.cinnamonpress.com

Designed and typeset in Bodini by Cinnamon Press. Cover design by Adam Craig from original artwork courtesy of Tom Bennett.

Cinnamon Press is represented by Inpress.

Acknowledgements

Grateful thanks to the editors who have published my work. Some of these poems have appeared in the following magazines and anthologies:

Acumen, Artemis, Binsted Competition Anthology, Brittle Star, Dempsey and Windle Competition Anthology, For the Silent: League Against Cruel Sports, Frogmore Papers, Locked Down: 2020 Pandemic Poems, Poems for the Year 2020: Eighty poets on the pandemic, Orbis, Poems in the Waiting Room, Poetry and All That Jazz, South, The Dawn Treader, U3AThird Age Magazine, Stanley Spencer Poems: An Anthology, Winchester Anthology.

I would like to thank the following people from the poetry workshops I attend, for their invaluable support: Pauline Hawkesworth, Jenny Hamlett, Richard Peirce, Richard Williams, Sue Spiers, Gareth Toms, Stephanie Norgate, Chris Sparks, Joan McGavin, Ruth Marden, Eve Jackson, Hugh Greasely, Mark Floyer, Lydia Fulleylove, Liz Neal, John Pearson, Richard Senior, Chris Martin, Mick Perryment, Jane Turner. Particular thanks go to Maggie Sawkins and Robyn Bolan who generously gave their time to read through my collection. Finally, special thanks to Jan Fortune at Cinnamon Press for her invaluable help and support in helping me nurture, and deliver *Things I have Kept.*

About the Author

Denise Bennett has an MA in creative writing and is widely published in poetry journals and has been placed in many poetry competitions. She has three collections: *Planting the Snow Queen* and *Parachute Silk* (Oversteps Books) and *Water Chits* (Indigo Dreams). She is a prize-winning poet, being the winner of the Poetry Society's inaugural Hamish Canham Prize. Most recently she won first prize in 2022 in the U3A (University of the Third Age), national poetry competition for her poem 'Jay' and was awarded second prize in the Southport Writers Circle poetry competition in 2023 for her poem 'Water Muscles'. She currently runs poetry and writing workshops in community settings, having taught creative writing for thirty years for Portsmouth College as part of their adult education programme. Much of her work is inspired by family events, local history, art work and nature. She has contributed many poems to The University of Portsmouth's Literary Map, an online interactive map created to highlight Portsmouth's impact on literature and inspire new writers. She always carries a notebook and pen to gather eaves-droppings and observations, the seeds for her poems.

Contents

to my mother, Ada Amelia Bailey 1912 – 2014

Things I Have Kept

Things I have kept

My air-force blue Biba maxi-coat
that swung me through the sixties,
and kept me warm;

the wooden pendant you fashioned
from ply wood, strung
on a fishing line—
early sign of love;

the newborn name-tags,
school uniform labels,
Emily Jane, Timothy James;
nested with cotton reels and cloth

in the sewing basket
you brought me back from Pitcairn,
woven from banana leaves,
which holds the haberdashery
of our marriage.

The Dance

for Tom—sculptor and husband

Your hands
have caught us on the hop,
in mid-step,
dancing the polka
on top of the bookcase—
flirting with our feet;

two stick-like
Giacomti figures.
We are not bronze
but fashioned from wire,
wrapped in gauze,
plastered, dusted with gold.

We lean into our marriage,
skip in 2/4 quick time,
have circled in courtship
for forty-nine years.
Please, don't let
the music stop.

Small Miracles

If truth be told
I'd settle for small miracles:

The song of the robin
on winter-dark mornings,

the first white lace
of the pear blossom in spring,

the cat curled asleep
on the porch in summer light,

the soft smoky-blue cloak
of dusk in autumn—

you and I drinking afternoon tea
on the lawn,

or spreading the presents
under the Christmas tree,

and the rhythm of the way
the world turns, and turns.

Virus

24th March 2020

All the world is reciting a prayer
this morning.

In my garden
the slender pear tree

puts on
her bridesmaid dress,

the magnolia raises her arms
fluttering white petaled gloves.

I hear the thrum of a mower
in the distance

reminding me
that life goes on.

Forget-me-nots

Covid 19 Death

After the rain
we walked the main road
to Langstone,

saw two black ribbons
of mourners lining
the verges, waiting

for the cortege;
watched as they waved
to the widow

when the hearse passed;
heard the whispers—
it was the virus,

a man and a woman,
he died, she survived.
We carried on down

the Billy line, saw
a brilliant crop of powder blue
forget-me-nots.

These Summer Evenings 2020

Inspired by Anglepoise by Paul Stephenson

he is in his workshop
working with wood,
turning the lathe

I am in my study
fretting over poems,
a comma, a dash;

the roses tremble
on the pergola—
a train rumbles past,

later, I will hold
the newly turned bowl,
he will read my words:

there will be blessings
of tea and lamplight—
everything will be fine.

Tulip Kiss

45th wedding anniversary 14th June 2020

he takes the wood
    in his arms

a bough fallen
    from a tulip tree

in the churchyard
    and with his

sculptor's hands
    fashions an image

of lovers
    caught in a near kiss

Sapphire Anniversary

Covid Celebration, 14th June 1975-2020

Outside the church
he sets up the tripod.

I sit on a bench like a new bride;
he stands behind

replicating our wedding shot;
he gets the light, the pose

just right—hold still, smile
we wait for the flash—

it's just the two of us today,
remembering the guests,

yellow roses, cream dress,
the tune of *Greensleeves,*

the notes of the nightingale
as we said our vows.

Walking

For Tom—summer 2020

We have brushed past
a tide of Queen Anne's Lace;
the powder of yellow-eyed
moon daisies has dusted
our clothes—

and I have loved our walks,
knowing that nothing matters more
than walking hand and hand
with you,
going home in the dusk.

Kindergarten 1

19th March 2020

Here is a festival of flowers;
children in a garden playing in winter drizzle,
or seated on logs, drinking milk,
holding on to each other, laughing.
The whole world is full of fear.

A-tishoo, a-tishoo, we all fall down.
I write a prayer in my notebook.
Please God, keep them safe.

Kindergarten 2

3rd June 2020

They have come out to play again
in soft summer rain. I hear their laughter;
the garden has been so silent.
I look through the trees
and pink dog-roses in the hedgerow,
to see them.

A-tishoo, a-tishoo, we all fall down.
I write again in my notebook.
Please God, keep them safe.

Pictures

Easter Sunday 12th April 2020

My son sends me a picture
of a Simnel cake
he has baked this Easter,
that we cannot share.
My daughter sends me a scene
from her balcony
full of red tulips
she has grown from seed—

and I carry these images
in my heart.
The fluency of their fingers
more precious than prayer.

You are not Icarus

I am glad you are not Icarus,
were never the high flyer,
had no wish to singe
your beautiful shiny wings.

You soar safely.
Your father has taught you well—

in all your fallings,
he has guided you,
given you sense enough
to seek easy landings

in fields of summer wheat,
or steered you on course
for sleeping sands
with soft waves to rock you—

even in your darkest flight
he gathered you in his arms,
opened his heart as wide
as a white silk parachute.

Soar safely, my son
your father has taught you well.

Protection

for Tim

That spring morning
when you rescued
the female blackbird,
trapped in the fruit cage,

when we set about
repairing torn nets
with a makeshift needle;
garden twine twisted

around a thin stick
dad handed us,
using giant green stitches
to cobble the holes,

our hands touching
as we passed the yarn
between us, inside to out;
working like weavers

to mend the mesh—
that spring morning,
we were never closer
listening to that blackbird
fling his notes into warm air.

Just for the Record

I've searched everywhere
for the immunisation records,
stashed in a safe place;

can recall the jabs they had:
whooping cough, diphtheria, rubella,
sugar cubes for polio;

can remember when my daughter,
too young for the vaccine,
caught measles; sponging the roses

from her skin as she screamed,
praying she would not go blind or die.
The doctor came everyday—

and I remember how croup
closed my son's throat
just before his first birthday;

the tube, his fists bound,
sitting by his critical, hospital cot
for a week, willing him to live—

the cards don't mention
the sweat, the struggle, the chapel,
those long, waiting hours,

those unpredictable vigils,
just the dates injections
were given, in neat black ink.

Separation

I remember
as if it were yesterday,
that primal scream
when we were finally torn apart—
the moment I first held
my bruised Scorpio daughter.

After she'd gone,
the bed had been stripped,
sheets neatly folded.
I stared at the bare mattress;
the place I used to lay her down,
the old rickety chair where
she would sit curled on my lap
and I would sing …

There were marks on the walls
where her posters had been;
ribbons of cellotape,
spots of Blu Tack, corner fragments
of torn pictures.
I ran my fingers
along her desk bereft of pens,
unlittered with papers and books.

A cardboard box held
things she no longer needed:
soft toys, cast-off clothes,
a cache of tiny, china cats
she used to collect …

and on the floor, discarded,
a pair of laceless, black ankle boots.
I closed the door.

Breathe, breathe,
I hear the midwife say.
Breathe, breathe—
it will pass …

Daughter

for Emily

I want to make you
a buttercup bracelet again,
to tell you the moon
is a slice of melon—
to translate all the stars
into your wishes.

Dear Sappho

I have a beautiful daughter, golden
Like a flower, my beloved Cleis

(fragment 75)

I have a beautiful daughter too,
with midnight hair;
grown to be a woman now.

I say she is gay which means
she is free to love whoever she loves,
just as you were—

but it wasn't always so.
Once there was a law which said
she would be unable to fly.

At school, bullies broke her wings
and I did not know how or why.
She did not speak for weeks ...

but the world is kinder now
and she has reached the sky
and soars where the lark sings.

Section 28, was introduced by Mrs Thatcher in 1988 which prohibited teachers
discussing same sex relationships.

Jay

She wishes to be known
by her new name now,

so I practice writing it
in sand and snow;

scribble it in black ink,
in steam on the window.

Although the midwife
handed me Emily Jane,

it's only a name I mourn
she is just the same;

happier now with Jay,
more neutral, more plain—

my grown-up daughter
with her new chosen name.

The Pairing of Larks

for my daughter

no guests
just two witnesses, she says

but gives me
the gift of time to find

white roses and ivy which,
in the language

of flowers, mean
friendship, fidelity, love

and I send these
with a blessing of lark-song—

sweet notes
rising like a prayer

Water Muscles

When she first learnt to swim
we put armbands on her

to keep her afloat, protect her.
Water muscles, she called them.

Later she swam in the sea;
a mermaid with a jet of wet, black hair.

At fifteen, the girls, the teachers,
let her flounder in the deep-end;

she almost drowned. The names they
called her for being gay, still hurt

to say. Her stoical life-jacket
pulled her through. The water muscles

saved her life. She could beat the bullies
hands down, in any gala now,

the young woman smiling
in her wedding photo with her wife.

Taking Down the Pear Tree

It should have been cut down
long ago but we've
let it straggle on.

Each year it puts out shoots
produces a head of blossom,
a small crop of fruit—juicy, sweet.

It even inspired a covid poem
I wrote when all the world
was sick, when I likened

it to a slender bride
dressed in white lace,
mainstay of fevered mornings;

a tide of scented flowers rising
like a prayer—but now
     it must be taken down.

My husband saws each limb,
leans them against the wall,
a cool, dry place to season,

digs out the trunk
no broader than a broom-stick,
finds the roots already rotted.

The tree has been dying these
last three years, shedding a pall
of buds, a plague-shroud.

Later, he makes a bookmark,
from wood sliced from the bark,
band-sawed, shaped, polished,

and the tree lives on
between pages of my poetry book
in the crook of my heart.

Mothering Sunday Lockdown 2020

for Tim, born Mothering Sunday 1982

When he turned up nearly a week early
with a box of chocolates and flowers
and said *I might not see you for awhile …*
It's like the Spanish Flu, Mum, thousands
are going to die—I was stunned. Later,
when the law decreed that we could not meet,
we waved in safety at the garden gate,
afraid. Plague-breath could kill us with a kiss.

Once a week we did the glove and mask dance
a good coffin's length away. That Easter
he baked a Simnel cake I could not eat;
texted a photo of this culinary treat.
All the while milky blackthorn spiked the sky,
we stood uncertain if we would live or die.

Requests

For Ada aged 101 and 5 months

She asks for brandy,
a chocolate éclair,
a new suit—flowered top and skirt
for when she gets up;
asks me to check
that her shoes are ready.

I say—
I will bring you brandy
and cake, buy you
a new pretty outfit.
I've checked to see
that your silver pumps are ready.

Dreckley

Dreckley she would say
in answer to all my 'when?' questions.
This might mean, soon, sometimes
in a while; I never really knew.
Dreckley was her fending off word.
I loved her language.

Put'un down she would say
if I fiddled with the kitten too long
Or *Where's it to?* whenever
she lost her hairbrush, purse, her comb.
Or *Where be that bey?*
if the paperboy were late,
or *be good maid,* if ever I was fretful.

Her roots were in the green folds
of her Devon hamlet,
her red-rich soil—
a world of sheep-bleats,
pony traps to markets,
butter and cream neighbours.

After her adventure to America,
emigrating when war-widowed,
she missed her country lanes.
I can just hear saying,
as she booked her passage home,

Ar've seen enough,
I be gwan 'ome noo, back to Deben.
In old age when sleep escaped her
she would sigh and say,
nigh'tarmes is always the worst.

When she died, I missed
the soft burr of her words.
Always, when visiting her grave
I lay flowers, touch her headstone,
blow a kiss.
See you dreckley I say.
See you dreckley

The Big Freeze

1962-63

It started on Boxing Day
with just a flurry of flakes.
Snow remained on the ground
for three months.
Sheets froze on the line,
streets were packed with ice.

There were few deliveries;
my mother trudged to the Co-op
to get coal or logs, lugged home
in a wheeled bag, to bank up the fire
in our cold prefab.
I remember her grit.

Today I wrap woollen socks,
and gloves, birthday gifts
for a grown-up daughter.
A mother's love will always
keep her child warm
no matter how old—
and wherever she is.

Speaking to my dead mother

What are we doing here in this station tearoom?
We've slipped back sixty years.
You're wearing your grey pencil-slim skirt,
queuing for the buffet. Sipping tea.
I'm in my pink cotton frock covered in smuts.
You'd told me not to sit facing the engine.
It's like old times, whiling away
minutes between steam trains—
each summer we took three to get to Devon.

I remember you telling me about that first time
we travelled. I was three weeks old,
you, fleeing from the baby snatchers
brandishing adoption forms.
How did you manage cases and a baby?
Did you feed me in the ladies waiting room?

I wish I could ask you how we sheltered
in a tearoom like this,
huddled like fugitives,
you afraid, running to the safety
of your family with your burden.
Mother, brother, sister.
Oh, but they took you in, didn't they?
And they took me in.
Before we say goodbye, I want to tell you
that each year, I still go back
to Devon to lay flowers.

Bruised Fruit

Rough market traders
often sold us rotten apples
from the back of the stall.

*Don't touch the front
It spoils the display.*
The sign said.

Each week we bought
bags of bruised fruit,
good enough for stewing.

In apple language
my mother would have
been a *Pink Lady,*

sweet, rouged cheeks,
toss of her glossy red hair,
but she'd been kicked about

a bit, like the stuff
at the back of the barrow—
but she was glad that

the apple-picker, thief—
the scrumper had deserted her,
leaving us to fend

for our own sugar
to sweeten our lives,
as much as we were able.

6 Shaftesbury Road

Maria Beadnell, Dickens' first lady-love
once lived here when the house was new;
when people entered by the flight of stone steps
up to the front door, in those *la-di-da* days.

Years later, as tenants, we entered
by a different door to the damp basement flat;
my mother bumping my pushchair
down to the squall of everyday living, below stairs—

those two gloomy rooms, shared scullery,
paint-peeling walls, where no sun shone.
Here she kept us safe, away from pointing
fingers—she a war widow left with a small son,

and me, her unexpected daughter.
We slept together in a big double bed.
If I went back, would I find my tiny thumb-prints
pressed into the door where I once fell,

gashing my head on the catch? I still
carry the scar from that place where
the maid once rose at six, broke the ice in the ewer
to wash, then carried up tea to Maria.

The Escalator

A contrapuntal poem

Sometimes I feel her standing next to me
in the department store;
I feel her take my hand
as we step onto the escalator;
remember how she taught me to ride safely,
to hold on tight and when to jump.
I can smell the scent on her clothes.

Learning to Fly

It's over sixty years since we both stood here
at the foot of the moving stairs.
She's all dolled up,
tailored suit, newly permed hair.
The fragrance of gardenia takes me back
to that first time I learnt to fly,
her gloved hand holding mine.

Flying with My Mother

Sometimes I feel her standing next to me;
　　it's over sixty years since we both stood here
in the department store,
　　at the foot of the moving stairs.
I feel her take my hand.
　　She's all dolled up,
as we step onto the escalator,
　　tailored suit, newly permed hair.
I remember how she taught me to ride safely;
　　the fragrance of gardenia takes me back—
—to hold on tight and when to jump—
　　to that first time I learnt to fly.
I can smell the scent on her clothes,
her gloved hand holding mine.

Christmas Swan

As I watch the pen glide upstream
carrying her cargo,
a bevy of cygnets balanced
on her back—
softly folded into her wings,
I remember one Christmas long ago—

a small, moulded, plastic swan,
in the snowy, Co-op window,
that I'd saved up pocket money
to buy for my mother;
the basket-shaped feathers
holding the precious, scented eggs.

Better by far

Better by far that you should forget and smile
than you should remember and be sad
Christina Rossetti 1830-1894

Today, in the Rock Garden
I remembered how we sat on the grass;
the scent of the pinks.

I saw you in your pencil skirt,
your red permed curls shining,
the slender stem of your neck;

remembered a hot summer day,
making a daisy chain,
you in white cotton gloves—

and, always the fine lady,
a scented lace hankie in your bag:
Elizabeth Arden's Blue Grass,

the fragrance takes me back.
I didn't remember it was
the anniversary of your death.

Foundling 453

A boy admitted 7th October 1748

When she dropped him
at the hospital

she tied a yellow ribbon
around his tiny wrist

with—
My name is Andrews

written in dark blue ink;
every letter an effort,

as if spelling out kinship
was more precious on cloth.

The strip, perhaps torn
from her special Sunday dress,

or a treasured fairing given
by her sweetheart,

was interleaved between
the pages of a large ledger…

Then they took him,
bathed him, swathed him

in uniform grey—
gave him a number—

and took his name away.

The Ship's Particulars

*On 22nd September 1883 'North' set sail for Australia
carrying English and Irish immigrants*

I read his name on the passenger list.
Daniel Cambridge, aged 22, single,
my great-grandfather,
'calling' Pattern Maker;
imagine his carpentry tools,
his home town, Athlone,
his memories of the potato plague.

He was billeted alongside
James, George, Thomas, Maurice
bricklayer, butcher, stone mason, carter,
from Clare, Derry, Cork,
each with their own trades,
bound for Australia.

From Dublin to Sydney
the voyage took 93 days,
late September, to Christmas Eve.
One child was born on the way,
six died—all recorded
in the ship's particulars
by the master.

Did he witness them, weighted
into their canvas bags,
hear the captain's prayers,
their mothers' cries
as they rocked them into the ocean?

Thirteen pounds, seven shillings
and sixpence was paid for each
immigrant worker.
Did he make good
in this wheat-scorched land?
Did he miss the kiss of Irish rain?
I read somewhere, that he came back.

The Irish Connection

for Judith

Today she flies out first class,
emigrates to Australia
the country she loves.

On the flight I will have my own shower,
snack-packs for when
I watch the films ...

We used to watch films
together, Wednesday afternoons
at the arts centre.

On our last meeting
I gave her a tiny button purse;
something light, a keepsake.

Sorry I didn't put a coin
in it for luck, your currency
will be different now.

I'll keep my silver sixpence
in it, the one the Catholic priest
blessed when I married;

it's an old Irish tradition
she explains. I hear her pain
of widowhood after

forty six years of marriage.
Now she will nestle
her coin in soft green leather.

Wishing you a safe journey,
Judith—
and a long and happy landing.

The Archer

The Mary Rose sank in 1545, was raised in 1982,
the archer was discovered in 1983

The day they raised the Mary Rose
I watched the cradle tilt,
the carcass almost slip
as I lifted my baby son
to witness history.
I stood roughly where Henry
had seen his ship sink.

Forty years on, I visit the museum,
stand before the figure of the archer.
They found him in the hold
lying on a woollen blanket
on top of ballast.
I imagine a fully-fleshed man
sleeping at the bottom of the sea.

Divers dredged up his skeleton.
Scientists examined his bones.
Technicians sculptured figure and face.
Historians dressed him
in leather jerkin, white shirt, woollen stockings,
concluded, he was a muscular man
with a twisted spine,
grooves in the bone of his bow-finger.

Five hundred men died
when the squall came,
the ship heeled, gun-ports unsealed,
let in the water,
trapped below by the death-nets,
a mesh spread across the decks
to prevent the French from boarding.
They could not cut the tar-coated ropes
with their knives.

Sometimes my son and I talk about
the loss, the drownings.
Somewhere in a drawer
I still have the shawl
I wrapped him in.

What the Osteoarchaeologist said

Footbones recovered from the Mary Rose which sank in 1545

They discovered a sack full
of sailors' shoes on the orlop deck;
a mixed bag of different sizes,
loose-fitting, slipper-style,
no lefts or rights;
found masses of footbones,
some still stuck to the leather.

It was such a humbling moment
handling history, she said—
to think that these
were just ordinary men
putting on their shoes
that morning.

HMS New Zealand

I tell my children *you are here*
because

in 1913 a Maori chief
gave the captain of HMS New Zealand
a piupiu, a skirt made from flax.

A ceremonial gift
with the prophecy that if worn
or kept close by in conflict

it would protect the ship
and crew—and his words were
remembered at the battles

of Dogger Bank, Heligoland Bight
and Jutland. It was the luckiest
ship they said. No loss of life

and because of this
a young bandsman, a flautist
called Francis survived

who had a son, who had
a daughter, who now stands
before the exhibition case

looking at the skirt displayed,
thinking of the tribal hands
that wove the leaves

which saved the sailors,
and how they'd grown the crop
from the seed of the flax.

Learning the Ropes

Slippery hitch, sheep shank, short splice,
halliards, hawsers—
even Nelson had to learn the ropes,
to know how to trim the sails;

and the sailmakers had to learn
how to cut the cloth slack so that
it would blow soft-bellied into the wind;

the weavers to interlace
warp and weft, the bare-foot mill-boy
to gather fluff from under machines—

and the spinners had to learn
how to heckle and comb the crop,
turn the fibres to linen,

the rope-makers how to twist
the strands to make the yarn,
to make the cable for the rigging—

and the pickers who gathered
flax for pennies, their children in tow,
had to know how to pull the roots.

It took twenty seven miles of rope
and four acres of canvas to sail the Victory—
all those hands along the way
learning the ropes.

Sailor Zoo

HMS Excellent, Whale Island—Portsmouth

There used to be a zoo here
at the Gunnery School, before the war.
A pets' palace, a paradise, depository
for the King's diplomatic gifts.

Exotic animals shipped
from far away lands, Australia, East Asia:
Kangaroos, monkeys, parrots
cast ashore by harassed captains.

Two polars, Nicholas and Barbara.
Two lionesses, Lola and Lorna
and a Russian bear called Baby;
a safe haven, enchantment for the staff

who learnt to rear wallaby and deer,
so different from handling weapons,
the routine of square bashing,
the pull of the field gun carriage.

Disbanded before the blitz came,
the animals were scattered, dispatched,
rehomed, never to feel again
the tenderness of a sailor's hand.

Day Raid

24th August 1940, 29 St Mary's Road Portsmouth

It was two o'clock in the afternoon
when we heard the siren wail;
in the living room,

James with his feet on the fender
thinking of the flicks, David,
Frank, Winifred and me drinking tea.

We scrambled for the Anderson
in our garden, grabbing
blankets, flasks and food.

Five hundred German bombers
came that day: eight kiddies killed
at the Princes Theatre. Our shelter

got a direct hit. All five of us died.
Then the mortuary squad arrived
shifting the rubble and found me

lying face down. Turning me over,
saw Pamela, six weeks old,
wrapped inside my thick coat,

whimpering, wounded, alive,
shrapnel embedded in her leg.
And they patched her up,

my orphaned daughter,
gave her a pension, ten bob a week,
wrote her name in a book,

sent her back to Gran.
And as the she grew older
the scar grew too, a legacy of war.

Irene

1938-2018

She never talked about it,
that last night
at 16 Cowper Road,
before the bomb dropped.

Lucy had just put the kettle on,
their married sister Lily
had popped in after shopping,
parked the pram in the hall.
They all sat chatting,
drinking tea in the front parlour,
mourning the death of their mother;
Mary and Ivy were knitting,
the baby sleeping.

She never said how long it took
the squad, scrabbling bare-handed
to dig the bodies from the rubble;
how Kathy had died
in the ambulance beside her,
Nellie, days later, in the next bed—

or how Tony, aged six months,
blown over a mile,
across roof-tops, was found dead
in a bed of nettles.
It took nearly a week
to find and identify him.
Just one small bump on his head.

She didn't remember the siren;
only the silence, the explosion,
the darkness.

She never talked about it,
her daughter said.

Selection—Auschwitz 1944

for Vera

Because the Hungarian girl
waiting, naked and shaved in the queue
understood a smattering of German,
when Dr Mengele pointed to her
distended belly and announced,

Schwanger—*pregnant.*
She retaliated
Ich bin doch eine Jungfrau,
Virgins couldn't be pregnant.
One small shrug, nod of his head
and she was sent to another line

to be starved, beaten, broken;
left too weary to grieve.
Years later, talking to her audience,
she said she bore no malice—
it was luck that she'd survived—

then said softly, when collecting
toys for a children's charity
in her working life,
how she'd flinched
when a cardboard box arrived
piled high with undressed dolls.

Haiku for Richard White

Musician Royal Marines Band 1893-1918

marble headstone
bright November sun—
falling leaves

I bend low
like a weeping willow
to read your name

on your grave
a white poppy flutters—
wind chills my bones

on my knees I breathe
scent of cut grass—
a musician lies here

Richard White sleeps
to the rumble of buses—
on home ground now

The Lace Makers

Many French prisoners of war held at Portchester Castle, Hants,
1794-1802, were lace makers

Bobbins were carved from meat-bones
stripped of flesh and bleached;
lathes shaped from dinner debris

and old wood. The bone workers
whittled away time while weavers
twisted linen and silk threads

around pinheads of the pattern,
creating delicate pillow-lace.
Sons who'd watched

their mothers work at home
taught the inmates their craft;
yards were sold at morning markets;

bartered for Nancy's fresh eggs,
Mary's milk or home-baked
loaves of bread. Women bore

away their booty to stitch
on collars, baby gowns, gathered
ruffles for cuffs until—jealous

of the prisoners' success—
village artisans complained.
Lace was confiscated, tools smashed,

masters and minions quashed,
but some resurrected their tools,
worked by moonlight, lace all the rage.

Dear Keats

Winchester

This soft September day
in clean, sharp air,
I followed your footsteps

past the Cathedral, the college,
the city gates, to that ancient place
they call Saint Cross.

I walked by the meadows
by the clear river
where cornfields winnowed

like a woman's hair.
Autumn has always been
a woman for me too:

The loaded bough,
drowsy bees, falling leaves,
the show of poppies.

I say, forget 'spoilt spring'
the shrill music of mating;
perpetual love calls,

give me a choir of swallows,
mournful cries of grown lambs;
the song of the robin.

St Agnes Eve

20th January 2019, Bedhampton Church

Ah, bitter chill it was!
                    The Eve of St Agnes, John Keats

By the light of the wintery St Agnes moon
laced through bare, black trees,
we picked our way past ancient graves
to the candle-lit poetry reading,
the chill of the village church
where Keats wrote his first and last lines
to fair Madeline.

Candles flickered as we listened
to the tale of how Porphyro
came to claim his sweet love, his ring dove—
and I, staring at the altar, remembered
when we had once knelt there to pray
and the nightingale that sang
in the trees on our wedding day.

Martha's Journal

The wife of the poet John Clare, July 1841

I found him by the roadside, feet bleeding.
Homesick, he said He'd walked eighty miles
from the asylum. He asked after Mary,
his long-ago sweetheart who died in a fire,
when a hot coal caught her cotton dress.
He fancied she was his first wife, poor lamb;
thought to see her running in the meadow,
daisies ribboning her hair. *Don't 'ee know me?*
I'm Martha, the milkmaid you married.
Your wife, Patty?' I led him in, bathed
his bruised legs. It was like the Bible story—
me the one who toiled, she, Mary,
the one in his head, who sat adoring.

Then he talked of Bessie, his dead sister,
the 'bonny' twin girl who died a few days
after her birth, while he, the weak one survived.
He spoke of her as a bud, innocent, unstained,
opening her pure white petals in heaven.

John, oh, my John!
I could not quell those voices in his head
Homesick. Homesick, he said.
I've walked many a weary mile
to see home in Mary's smile.

I took him in my arms, rocked him,
those wild demons threshing his brain.
Bide quiet John, bide quiet, I said.
I could still see the flash of madness
in his eyes. Then he lay on the bed
and slept, he slept, slept like a child.

What Tess said

That morning I rose at dawn,
and dressed as a harvest hand,

put on my cotton bonnet and jacket,
gloves to stop the shocks cutting

my flesh, danced with the other girls
under a lark-song sky—our movements

like a corn-gathering quadrille,
as we bent and stooped to bind the sheaves,

embracing the stooks like lovers—
my breasts brimming with milk.

At noon my sister Liza brought
my son and I unbuttoned my dress,

watched his perfect mouth open like
like a wet, pink rose to suckle;

his tiny hands weaving the air
and I kissed him and kissed him again,

called him my own dear sweeting.
Then Liza took him home

and I went on binding the sheaves
in the heat-haze until the moon rose.

That night he sickened, no priest
or doctor came and I baptised him *Sorrow*

just before he died, using the ewer
from the washstand to wet his head.

Next evening I stole out in the dark;
carried him like doll in a box—

buried him where the nettles grow
on the north side of the cemetery,

remembering that golden harvest day
when I held him close...

Reading Larkin to Rosemary

Haibun

We are visiting a dying friend. She is lying on her side, eyes shut tight. *Talk to her,* her husband says. *She can hear you.* We kiss her, say her name. *Hello, Rosemary;* sit and chat, sip tea, as if we are just three women in a café, catching up. *I remember when you went to Greenham Common. We hear your granddaughter qualified to be a midwife. You once told me how you taught your students the sorrow of The Somme* ... I know she likes Larkin so her husband fetches her poetry book and we begin to read to her, selecting *The Whitsun Weddings.* We each read a stanza, sharing a pair of reading glasses as we pass the book. When, we exchange the glasses we say *We're just swapping glasses, Rosemary.* We laugh at the silliness of this; hoping she enjoys the joke. Her eyes-lids tremble. After we have exhausted the scenes of *The Whitsun Weddings;* the poet describing guests on station platforms from the carriage window; bridesmaids in lemons and mauves, *whoops and skirls* of skittish girls, confettied couples kissing, and cinemas and churches as the train rattled by, I find a favourite quiet poem, 'The Trees'.

outside her window
grey February sky—
snowdrops on the path

Shaking the Soil from Your Shoulders

after The Resurrection, Cookham by Stanley Spencer

It's early morning in the churchyard.
Everyone is rising from their box graves,
untying green-starred ribbons of ivy.
Everywhere I hear the crack of stone.

Boat-loads of trippers
are swanning up the river. One has landed,
the other is jazzed along by a honky-tonk piano;
villagers racket around with pots and pans.

The bells are ringing a quarter peel
while Stanley, Stanley stands naked
surveying the scene, his feet planted
in a tickle of pale moon-daisies.

The roof of the church porch is awash
with a tide of white roses,
a Madonna figure sits nursing
three babies and kids swing on the kissing gate

and I am the woman, the woman in the brown dress
brushing down your jacket,
shaking the soil from your shoulders,
that intimate thing that only a lover will do.

Listening From Punts

after Christ preaching at Cookham Regatta by Stanley Spencer

Dear Stanley

I love your four ladies dancing in a punt.
One in a gypsy-swish skirt who jumps a rope,
one who scuffles her feet on a velvet cloth,
another stamping, Spanish-style, on a flat fish,
and I can almost hear a brass band
umph-pah-pah-ing up the river
as a sea-nymph lady grabs a bloke in a blazer and boater
as she listens to the sermon.

Follow me—and I will make you fishers of men.

But Stanley,
Christ didn't call women did he?
They had to be Mary or Martha,
sit at home by the hearth
with their jars of oil,
preparing the bread and wine—

but they can be priests now, Stanley.
Lately ordained, they can trawl,
cast their nets wide, catch
and haul home shoals of drowning souls.
They can marry and bury, confirm,
console…

How would you paint them today?
Rows and rows of dog-collared
women in long black robes;
just a scrap of lace and red pumps
showing beneath their cassocks.

Shrines

after Washing Lockers by Stanley Spencer

Kneeling here in the bathroom,
wedged between two magenta tubs—
pinned into sackcloth apron,
I could almost be saying a prayer
while the other orderlies follow the call
of carbolic, scour hospital lockers—
wash away the stains of war.
Here in this sacred space,
I'm taking time out from the wounded,
those avenues of iron bedsteads,
red and white blossom of flesh.

I find comfort in cleanliness,
the brisk rub of soap on wood grain so different
from gentle dabs of swabs on skin.
These temples are temporary homes
for Tommy's treasures: The water jug,
drinking cup. Stuff from home:
photos, letters, fags, stubs of pencils,
the daywear *hospital blues* neatly folded;
something to do in quiet times,
a book, a paper, perhaps a pack of cards
for playing patience.

As I kneel here quietly in ward four
I think of the men patched up,
sent back, as we scrub their
life-prints away, their personal effects
pocketed in uniforms again—small things
carried into battle, returned to families,
relics of war re-housed in other shrines now:
sideboards, cupboards, bedside tables—
and I think of those who will sleep
in rows again, their white headstones
which someone else will keep clean.

A Parasol Afternoon

after A Corner of the Artist's Room by Gwen John

I am happy here
in my Paris attic studio,
airy, light, my table
graced with scented flowers.

Here, I listen for weather,
see rain-shine roof-tops
through the misty lens
of lace curtains,

sit in my wicker chair,
snug in my blue shawl,
swathed about my shoulders;
wait for the sky to clear,

ready to unfurl
my white sun umbrella
and step out into
the parasol afternoon.

Cabbage Patch

After the painting, The Cabbage Field by Edward King 1862-1951

I step out from the ward
into the quiet afternoon—
load my brush to paint
the thin, white, drum-skin sky
that stretches far away

to the house on the hill—
start to paint the cabbage field,
vegetables laid out in tight rows
like the hospital bedsteads,
so close, we scrabble up from the foot
to climb in. No space to pray.

By day, patients come
in their rough grey uniforms
to till the field, free
to take a daily dose of salty air.
Warmed by the sun,
buffeted by the wind, they sing.

*

Today surveyors tramp the site
in hi-vis jackets, hard hats,
with measuring sticks, theodolites,
clipboards—busy making plans
for executive houses.

No one remembers the farm now:
the thatched barn,
row of cool, cypress trees,
potting sheds, the piggery,
cabbage patch—
patient's hands that worked the land.

*Edward King was a patient at St James' psychiatric hospital, Portsmouth for over
25 years. During WW2 he was the city's war artist and painted many scenes of the
blitz damage. He also painted the grounds of the hospital.*

Stray

after the tapestry The Man and his Best Friend
by Aran Alsworth, textile artist,

She has stitched him
in coloured, cotton thread;
image of the homeless man
on the pavement;

black beanie hat,
puffer jacket, nursing
a dog as if it were his child;

worked her needle
from a photograph, inking
his tattooed hands

that beg for bread.—
spare some change please,
something for my dog.

He knows what love is now;
the touch of fur,
a warm body held close,
a heartbeat, a heartbeat, a heartbeat …

The Sitter

After the painting of Mrs Clement Cross by Glyn Philpot

He has dressed me up like a magpie,
seated me on a zebra cushion,
made me wear a black-fringed shawl
snaking over my left shoulder.

I have been preened into this pose,
a swag of ermine lights my face.
I hold the opals in my eyes,
try not cry, hands tense inside silk gloves;

my scented lips are pursed like closed
pink rose petals. He has caged me with his brush,
just a light dust of blush on my cheeks.
Oh, those lovely bones, he'd said.

It was just a charade to him, fun,
family flying around the room
fetching props, an artistic drama—
and did he have to hedge-trim my hair?

Scene

Inspired by It's Raining Art, by John Boyes

It's a prize winner,
this moment, held in your hand;
click of the shutter.

No scrap of cream lace,
posy of yellow roses,
no tide of green lawn,

only figures in silhouette
under the wet trees,
hoop of white lights;

standing black statues,
backs to the camera,
brollies joshing,

the wet shine of earth
singing in the lens.
Yet, there could be a bride

in a taffeta pencil-dress,
the focus of attention
far beyond your eye.

Plough

Inspired by Ploughing Match image by Chris Dixon

Husbands of my great aunts,
men whose forebears
had tilled the red Devon soil,

toiled for hundreds of years,
harnessed their horses
in all weathers, browband, headpiece,

readied their shires under
delphinium blue or platinum skies,
laboured to steer their heavy beasts,

slicing iron-hard earth
as the wheel of the season turned,
or sweltered in summer heat,

watched as feathered fetlocks
brushed the harvest wheat;
these men who sang at Evensong

in the church choir
and prayed loudly each Sunday
for their daily bread—

weekdays poised at the plough,
when there was no work,
left their way of life, their wives,

in search of better things—
went to the prairies of America,
land of their dreams, and—

worked on farms and land,
established new homes
before they sent for their brides.

Prometheus Plays with Clay

Put down your fire, Prometheus,
and make a maquette of man.

First bend some thin wire
to shape the skeleton;
rib-cage, knee-caps, pelvis.

Then take your warm clay,
remember to let your hands dance
as you cover the bones.

Put down your fire, Prometheus,
and make a maquette of man.

Feel the texture beneath
your fingers, the soft slip
as you twist the limbs;

use your spatula and rake
to create the head—make it
more beautiful than your own.

Put down your fire, Prometheus,
and make a maquette of man.

Fashion a model of life
and energy—make his shoulders
strong enough to bare

the weight of the world.
Give him joy, sorrow and hope,
arms to embrace love.

Put down your fire, Prometheus,
and make a maquette of man.

By the lake

People sit on benches
quiet as choristers
in choir stalls
before the first hymn.

Beside the reed-bed
purple loosestrife
rise like candle flames.

Overhead, leaves rustle
in vaulted branches.
A blackbird opens his throat
and sings.

Irises

Here in the Quaker silence,
I file words away in my head;
and stare at the jar of blue irises
picked from a January garden.

These flowers know all there
is to know about love and loss and grief
just as I know how to mark out
the minutes of the Meeting,

the time for me to keep silent
and the time to speak.

The Running of the Deer

Born with the love of the land
and animals, my uncle,
a gentle lad of Exmoor,
hated to watch the hunt;
loved to see the red deer running free.

It wasn't easy then, he said.
When I worked for the Squire
I had to run with the hounds
or lose my job.
There were younger brothers and sisters
at home to feed.

At the end of the chase
when the stag ran panting
tired, torn and bleeding,
he would stop his ears…

Years later, unfettered,
he wrote endless letters
to the newspapers campaigning
against this cruel blood sport—

thoughts of white spotted fawns,
of hinds grazing at dawn,
the majesty of the stag,
always in his heart.

Geoffrey's Funeral

28th April 2023

We have been asked to bring
garden flowers.
I select yellow tulips,
forget-me-nots, bluebells,
orange blossom,
twist with tendrils of ivy,
tie with string.
At the grave side
the birds sing.

He cometh up, and is cut down,
like a flower …

Suffragette Garden

My neighbour sits reading
in her September garden
of suffragette colours:

white spiky chrysanthemums,
slender wands of purple phlox,
a mass of wispy greenery;

a second wind of wisteria
hangs from the trellis.
This afternoon she called me

in to see her morning glory
leaning against the fence, petals
furled in cooling air.

I'm training them your way,
she says, pointing to the strings.
Each day I watch from my window

to witness twisted tendrils,
see the choir of blue stars
crowning my garden wall—

the funnel shaped flowers
a triumph over adversity.

December Garden

A flock of long-tailed tits arrive
on a chill winter day; a string of birds,
black and white, blush-breasted,
with puff-ball bodies.

The ring leader balances
on the top-most olive branch,
tap, tap tapping at my window,
the quiver of his rump, a shut fan.

His dance on the glass shows
a narcissistic reflection.
Is he dreaming of the nest
he will make, lined with wool,

soft moss, spider-silk, lichen,
finished with a duvet of feathers—
for the white eggs, speckled rust-red,
that his hen will lay?

Robin's Song

In the holiness of this brief moment
a bright soprano star sings in the sky;
the robin's song on the cradle is spent
in the holiness of this brief moment—
and the sleeping baby seems so content
with this winter carol, his lullaby.
In the holiness of this brief moment
a bright soprano star sings in the sky.